THE UPANISHAD : A KEY TO INDIAN SPIRITUALITY

GOLU KUMAR

Contents

ONE

There are between one hundred fifty and one hundred seventy "Upanishads," according to estimates. The earliest of them are thought to have been created around 600 B.C., which is before the Buddha's ascendance. They are made up of numerous discourses on the immortality of the soul, the nature of man, the Supreme Being, and the nature of man. They are a part of Sanskrit Brahmanic literature and, in contrast to conventional truth, have the authority of revelation. In these works, we observe how the human mind tries to understand God and the purpose of man. The outcome is the development of clear theosophy,

in which we find the Brahman in his meditation trusting to the intuitions of his spirit, the promptings of his reason, or the combinations of his fancy, for a revelation of the truth. The result is given to us in these wonderful books. We call them wonderful, because the unaided mind of man never attained, in any other literature, a more profound insight into spiritual things. The Western reader may find in an "Upanishad" many things that seem to him trifling and absurd, many things obscure and meaningless. It is very easy to ridicule this kind of literature. But these ancient writings well repay study, as the most astounding productions of the human intellect. In them we see the human mind wrestling with the greatest thoughts that had ever yet dawned upon it, and trying to grasp and measure the mighty vision before which it was humbled to the dust. The seer, to communicate to the world the result of his meditations, seems to catch at every symbol and every word hallowed by familiar usage, to set out in concrete shape the color and dimensions of mystic verities; he is employing an old language for the expression of new truths; he is putting new wine into old wine-skins, which burst and the wine is spilled; words fail, and the meaning is lost. It is not lost, however, to those who will try to study the "Upanishads" from within, and not from without who will try to put themselves in the attitude of those earnest and patient explorers who brought so much light into the human life of the East, and so much joy and tranquillity to the perturbed spirit of their fellow-men. Those who thus study these ancient writings will find in them the fundamental principles of a definite theology, and, more wonderful still, the beginnings of that which became afterward known to the Greeks, and has been known ever since, as metaphysics: that is, scientific transcendentalism. This much will be apparent to anyone who will read and study the "Kaushîtaki- Upanishad," which is one of the most wonderful religious books of the East. Laying aside the doctrine of metempsychosis and the idea of reincarnation, there is something sublime and inspiring in the imagery with which the destiny of the soul after death is described, while in the metaphysical subtlety of this book we find an argument against materialism which is just as fresh now as when it was first stated.

KAUSHÎTAKI-UPANISHAD

THE BRAHMAN COUCH.

To carry out a sacrifice, Kitra Gângyâyani appointed Runi Uddâlaka as his head priest. However, Runi instructed his son Svetaketu to make the sacrifice on his behalf. "Son of Gautama, is there a hidden location in the world where you can position me, or is it the other way, and are you going to place me in the world to which that other way leads?," Kitra questioned Svetaketu when he arrived.

He responded by saying: "I am not aware of this. Let me, however, seek the master."
After approaching his father, he said, "So Kitra has asked me; how shall I respond?"

Runi stated: "I am likewise ignorant about this. We won't be able to get what other people provide us, i.e. wisdom until we have learned the correct portion of the Veda in Kitra's own home. Come, and we'll both leave."

After stating this, he walked up to Kitra Gângyâyani and said, "May I come close to you?" like a student. He answered: "Gautama, you are deserving of Brahman since you did not let pride drive you astray.
Come here, and I'll explain everything to you."

And Kitra said: "All who depart from this world go to the moon. In the former, the bright half, the moon delights in their spirits; in the other, the dark half, the moon sends them on to be born again. Verily, the moon is the door of the Svarga, i.e., the heavenly world. Now, if a man objects to the moon and is not satisfied with life there, the moon sets him free. But if a man does not object, then the moon sends him down as rain upon this earth. And according to his deeds and according to his knowledge he is born again here as a worm, or as an insect, or as a fish, or as a bird, or as a lion, or as a boar, or as a serpent, or as a tiger, or as a man, or as something else in different places. When he has thus returned to the earth, someone, a sage, asks: 'Who art thou?' And he should answer: 'From the wise moon, who orders the seasons, when it is born consisting of fifteen parts, from the moon who is the home of our ancestors, the seed was brought. This seed, even me, they, the gods, mentioned in the Pañkâgnividyâ, gathered up in an active man, and through an active man, they brought me to a mother. Then I, growing up to be born, a being living by months, whether twelve or thirteen, was together with my father, who also lived by years of twelve or thirteen months, that I might either know the true Brahman or not know it. Therefore, O ye seasons, grant that I may attain immortality, i.e., knowledge of Brahman. By this my true saying, by this my toil, beginning with the dwelling in the moon and ending with my birth on earth, I am like a season and the child of the seasons.' 'Who art thou?' the sage asks again. 'I am thou,' he replies. Then he sets him free to proceed onward.

"He, at the time of death, having reached the path of the gods, comes to the world of Agni, or fire, to the world of Vâyu, or air, to the world of Varuna, to the world of Indra, to the world of Pragâpati, to the world of Brahman. In that world, there is the lake Âra, the moments called Yeshtiha, the river Vigarâ, i.e., age-less, the tree Ilyâ, the city Sâlagya, the palace Aparâgita, i.e., unconquerable, the door-keepers Indra and Pragâpati, the hall of Brahman, called Vibhu (built by Vibhu, egoism), the throne Vikakshanâ, i.e., perception, the couch Amitaugas or endless splendor, and the beloved Mânasî, i.e., mind, and her image Kâkshushî, the eye, who, as if taking flowers, are weaving the worlds, and the Apsaras, the Ambâs, or sacred scriptures, and Ambâyavîs, or understanding, and the rivers Ambayâs leading to the knowledge of Brahman. To this world he who knows the Paryanka-vidyâ approaches. Brahman says to him: 'Run towards him, servants, with such worship as is due to me. He has reached the river Vigarâ, the age-less, he will never age.'

"Then five hundred Apsaras go towards him, one hundred with garlands in their hands, one hundred with ointments in their hands, one hundred with perfumes in their hands, one hundred with garments in their hands, one hundred with fruit in their hands. They adorn him with an adornment worthy of Brahman, and when thus adorned with the adornment of Brahman, the knower of Brahman moves towards Brahman. He comes to the lake Âra, and he crosses it by the mind, while those who come to it without knowing the truth, are drowned. He comes to the moment called Yeshtiha, they flee from him. He comes to the river Vigarâ and crosses it by the mind alone, and there shakes off his good and evil deeds. His beloved relatives obtain the good, his unbeloved relatives the evil he has done. And as a man, driving in a chariot might look at the two wheels without being touched by them, thus he will look at day and night, thus at good and evil deeds, and at all pairs, all correlative things, such as light and darkness, heat and cold. Being freed from good and freed from evil, he, the knower of Brahman, moves towards Brahman.

"He approaches the tree Ilya, and the odor of Brahman reaches him. He approaches the city of Sâlagya, and the flavor of Brahman reaches him. He approaches the palace Aparâgita, and the splendor of Brahman reaches him. He approaches the doorkeepers Indra and Pragâpati, and they run away from him. He approaches the hall Vibhu, and the glory of Brahman reaches him and he thinks, 'I am Brahman.' He approaches the throne Vikakshanâ. The Sâman verses, Brihad and Rathantara, are the eastern feet of that throne; the Sâman verses, Syaita and Naudhasa, its western feet; the Sâman verses, Vairûpa and Vairâga, its sides lengthways, south and north; the Sâman verses,

Sâkvara and Raivata, its sides crossways, east and west. That throne is Pragñâ, knowledge, for, by knowledge, self-knowledge, he sees clearly. He approaches the couch Amitaugas. That is Prâna, i.e., speech. The past and the future are its eastern feet; prosperity and the earth are its western feet; the Sâman verses, Brihad and Rathantara, are the two sides lengthways of the couch, south, and north; the Sâman verses, Bhadra and Yagñâyagñiya, are its cross-sides at the head and feet, east and west; the Rik and Sâman are the long sheets, east and west; the Yagus the cross-sheets, south, and north; the moon-beam the cushion; the Udgîtha the white coverlet; prosperity the pillow. On this couch sits Brahman, and he who knows himself one with Brahman, sitting on the couch, mounts it first with one foot only. Then Brahman says to him: 'Who art thou?' and he shall answer: 'I am like a season, and the child of the seasons, sprung from the womb of endless space, from the light, from the luminous Brahman. The light, the origin of the year, which is the past, which is the present, which is all living things, and all elements, is the Self. Thou art the Self. What thou art, that am I.' Brahman says to him: 'Who am I?' He shall answer: 'That which is, the truth.' Brahman asks: 'What is the truth?' He says to him: 'What is different from the gods and from the senses that is Sat, but the gods and the senses are Team. Therefore, by that name Sattya, or true, is called all this whatever there is. All this thou art.' This is also declared by a verse: 'This great Rishi, whose belly is the Yagus, the head the Sâman, the form the Rik, is to be known as being imperishable, as being Brahman.'

"Brahman says to him: 'How dost thou obtain my male names?' He should answer: 'By breath.' Brahman asks: 'How are my female names?' He should answer: 'By speech.' Brahman asks: 'How are my neuter names?' He should answer: 'By mind.' 'How smells?' 'By the nose.' 'How forms?' 'By the eye.' 'How sounds?' 'By the ear.' 'How flavors of food?' 'By the tongue.' 'How actions?' 'By the hands.' 'How pleasures and pain?' 'By the body.' 'How joy, delight, and offspring?' 'By the organ.' 'How journeyings?' 'By the feet.' 'How thoughts, and what is to be known and desired?' 'By knowledge alone.'

"Water is certainly my world—all of Brahman's world—and it is thine, says Brahman to him.

Whoever knows this, yea, who knows this, obtains whatsoever victory, whatever might be ascribed to Brahman.

AN UNDERSTANDING OF THE LIVING SPIRIT.

Kaushîtaki adds, "Prâna, or breath, is Brahman." The mind is the messenger, speech is the housewife, the sight is the guard, and the ear is the informant of this prâna, which is Brahman. He becomes seized by the message when he recognizes the mind as the representative of prâna, which is Brahman. Whoever speaks in the housekeeper's voice takes on the housekeeper's characteristics. Whoever recognizes the eye as the guard is taken over by the guard. When someone recognizes an ear as an informant, they take on that person's characteristics.

"Now to that prâna, which is Brahman, all these deities, mind, speech, eye, ear, bring an offering, though he asks not for it, and thus to him who knows this all creatures bring an offering, though he asks not for it. For him who knows this, there is this Upanishad or secret vow, 'Beg not!' As a man who has begged through a village and got nothing sits down and says, 'I shall never eat anything given by those people,' and as then those who formerly refused him press him to accept their alms, thus is the rule for him who begs not, but the charitable will press him and say, 'Let us give to thee.'"

"Prâna, or breath, is Brahman," thus says Pangya. "And in that prâna, which is Brahman, the eye stands firm behind speech, the ear stands firm behind the eye, the mind stands firm behind the ear, and the spirit stands firm behind the mind. To that prâna, which is Brahman, all these deities bring an offering, though he asks not for it, and thus to him who knows this, all creatures bring an offering, though he asks not for it. For him who knows this, there is this Upanishad or secret vow, 'Beg not!' As a man who has begged through a village and got nothing sits down and says, 'I shall never eat anything given by those people,' and as then those who formerly refused him press him to accept their alms, thus is the rule for him who begs not, but the charitable will press him and say, 'Let us give to thee.'

"Now follows the attainment of the highest treasure, i.e., spirit. If a man meditates on that highest treasure, let him on a full moon or a new moon, or in the bright fortnight, under an auspicious Nakshatra, at one of these proper times, bending his right knee, offer oblations of ghee with a ladle, after having placed the fire, swept the ground, strewn the sacred grass, and sprinkled water. Let him say: 'The deity called Speech is the attainer, may it attain this for me from him who possesses and can bestow what I wish for. Svâhâ to it!' 'The deity called prâna, or breath, is the attainer, may it attain this for me from him. Svâhâ to it!' 'The deity called the eye is the attainer, may it attain this for me from him. Svâhâ to it!' 'The deity called the ear is the attainer, may it attain this for me from him. Svâhâ to it!' 'The deity called mind is the attainer of it, may it attain this for me from him. Svâhâ to it!' 'The deity called knowledge is the attainer of it, may it attain this for me from him. Svâhâ to it!'

"Then having inhaled the smell of the smoke, and having rubbed his limbs with the ointment of ghee, walking on in silence, let him declare his wish, or let him send a messenger. He will surely obtain his wish.

"Now follows the Daiva Smara, the desire to be accomplished by the gods. If a man desires to become dear to any man or woman, or any men or women, then at one of the fore-mentioned proper times he offers, in the same manner as before, oblations of ghee, saying: 'I offer thy speech in myself, I this one here, Svâhâ.' 'I offer thy ear in myself, I this one here, Svâhâ.' 'I offer thy mind in myself, I this one here, Svâhâ.' 'I offer thy knowledge in myself, I this one here, Svâhâ.' Then having inhaled the smell of the smoke, and having rubbed his limbs with the ointment of ghee, walking on in silence, let him try to come in contact or let him stand speaking in the wind, so that the wind may carry his words to the person by whom he desires to be loved. Surely he becomes dear, and they think of him.

"Now follows the restraint instituted by Pratardana, the son of Divodâsa: they call it the inner Agnihotri. So long as a man speaks, he cannot breathe, he offers all the while his breath in his speech. And so long as a man breathes, he cannot speak, he offers all the while his speech in his breath. These two endless and immortal oblations he offers always, whether waking or sleeping. Whatever other oblations there are (those, e.g., of the ordinary Agni-hotri, consisting of milk and other things), they have an end, for they consist of works which, like all works, have an end. The ancients, knowing this the best Agni-hotri, did not offer the ordinary Agnihotri.

"Uktha is Brahman, thus said Sushkabhringâra. Let him meditate on the uktha as the same with the Rik, and all beings will praise him as the best. Let him meditate on it as the same with the Yagus, and all beings will join before him as the best. Let him meditate on it as the same with the Sâman, and all beings will bow before him as the best. Let him meditate on it as the same with might, let him meditate on it as the same with glory, let him meditate on it as the same with splendor. For as the bow is among weapons the mightiest, the most glorious, the most splendid, thus is he who knows this among all beings the mightiest, the most glorious, the most splendid. The Adhvaryu conceives the fire of the altar, which is used for the sacrifice, to be himself. In it, the Adhvaryu weaves the Yagus portion of the sacrifice. And in the Yagus portion, the Hotri weaves the Rik portion of the sacrifice. And in the Rik portion, the Udgâtri weaves the Sâman portion of the sacrifice. He, the Adhvaryu, or prâna, is the self of the threefold knowledge; he indeed is the self of prâna. He who knows this is the self of it, i.e., becomes prâna.

"Next follows the three kinds of meditation of the all-conquering Kaushîtaki. The all-conquering Kaushîtaki adores the sun when rising, having put on the sacrificial cord, having brought water, and having thrice sprinkled the water cup, saying: 'Thou art the deliverer, deliver me from sin.' In the same manner, he adores the sun when in the zenith, saying: 'Thou art the highest deliverer, deliver me highly from sin.' In the same manner, he adores the sun when setting, saying: 'Thou art the full deliverer, deliver me fully from sin.' Thus he fully removes whatever sin he committed by day and by night. And in the same manner, he who knows this likewise adores the sun and fully removes whatever sin he committed by day and by night.

"Then, secondly, let him worship every month in the year at the time of the new moon, the moon as it is seen in the west in the same manner as before described the sun, or let him send forth his speech towards the moon with two green blades of grass, saying: 'O thou who art mistress of immortal joy, through that gentle heart of mine which abides in the moon, may I never weep for misfortune concerning my children.'

"The offspring of him who thus reveres the moon do not pass away before him. So it is with a father who has previously given birth to a son.

"On to the person whose son has not yet been born. He murmurs the three verses of Rik. "Growth, O Soma! "May milk and food come to thee." "That beam which the dityas gladden." "May vigor come to thee."

"Having muttered these three Rik verses, he says: 'Do not increase by our breath, by our offspring, by our cattle; he who hates us and whom we hate, increase by his breath, by his offspring, by his cattle. Thus I turn the turn of the god, I return the turn of Âditya.' After these words, having raised the right arm towards Soma, he lets it go again.

"Then, thirdly, let him worship on the day of the full moon the moon as it is seen in the east in the same manner, saying: 'Thou art Soma, the king, the wise, the five-mouthed, the lord of creatures. The Brahmana is one of thy mouths; with that mouth, thou eatest the kings; make me an eater of food by that mouth! The king is one of thy mouths; with that mouth thou eatest the people; make me an eater of food by that mouth! The hawk is one of thy mouths; with that mouth, thou eatest the birds; make me an eater of food by that mouth! Fire is one of thy mouths; with that mouth thou eatest this world; make me an eater of food by that mouth! In thee there is the fifth mouth; with that mouth thou eatest all beings; make me an eater of food by that mouth! Do not decrease by our life, by our offspring, by our cattle; he who hates us and whom we hate, decrease by his life, by his offspring, by his cattle. Thus I turn the turn of the god, I return the turn of Âditya.' After these words, having raised the right arm, he lets it go again.

"Next, having addressed these prayers to Soma, when being with his wife, let him stroke her heart, saying: 'O fair one, who hast obtained immortal joy by that which has entered thy heart through Pragâpati, mayest thou never fall into sorrow about thy children.' Her children then do not die before her.

"Next, if a man has been absent and returns home, let him kiss his son's head, saying: 'Thou springest from every limb, thou art born from the heart, thou, my son, art my self indeed: live thou a hundred harvests.' He gives him his name, saying: 'Be thou a stone, be thou an ax, be thou solid gold; thou, my son, art light indeed: live thou a hundred harvests.' He pronounces his name. Then he embraces him, saying: 'As Pragâpati the lord of creatures embraced his creatures for their welfare, thus I embrace thee,' (pronouncing his name). Then he mutters into his right ear, saying: 'O thou, quick Maghavan, give to him.' 'O Indra, bestow thy best wishes'--thus he whispers into his left ear. Let him then thrice kiss his head, saying: 'Do not cut off the line of our race, do not suffer. Live a hundred harvests of life; I kiss thy head, O son, with thy name.' He then thrice makes a lowing sound over his head, saying: 'I low over thee with the lowing sound of cows.'

"Next follows the Daiva Parimara, the dying around of the gods, the absorption of the two classes of gods, mentioned before, into prâna or Brahman. This Brahman shines forth indeed when the fire burns, and it dies when it burns not. Its splendor goes to the sun alone, the life prâna, the moving principle, to the air.

This Brahman does come to life when the sun is visible, and it perishes when it is not. Its beauty belongs only to the moon, and its life to the air.

This Brahman does come to life when the moon is visible, and it perishes when it is not. The only source of its magnificence and life is the lightning.

This Brahman does indeed shine when the lightning strikes, but it perishes when it does not. Its beauty and life are transferred to the air.

"Thus all these deities (fire, sun, moon, lightning), having entered the air, though dead, do not vanish; and out of the very air, they rise again. So much concerning the deities. Now then, concerning the body.

"This Brahman truly comes into being when one talks, and it perishes when one does not. His beauty is only for the eye, and his life is for breathing.

When one sees with the eye, this Brahman truly shines; nevertheless, when one does not perceive, it fades. Its beauty is only audible, which gives life.

When one hears with the ear, this Brahman does indeed flash forth; yet, when one does not hear, it dies. Only the mind, the life to breathe, can appreciate its grandeur.

"When one thinks with the mind, this Brahman truly shines, and when one doesn't think, it disappears. Its beauty belongs to the breath and the life alone.

"As a result, despite being dead after entering life or breath alone, all these deities (the senses, etc.) do not disappear; rather, they emerge again from the same breath. Furthermore, even if the southern and northern mountains tried to crush the man who knows this, they would fail. However, those who despise him and those who he despises perish in his vicinity.

"Next follows the Nihsreyasâdâna, i.e., the accepting of the preeminence of breath or life by the other gods. The deities, speech, eye, ear, mind, contending with each for who was the best, went out of this body, and the body lay without breathing, withered, like a log of wood. Then speech went into it, but speaking by speech, it lay still. Then the eye went into it, but speaking by speech, and seeing by the eye, it lay still. Then the ear went into it, but speaking by speech, seeing by the eye, hearing by the ear, it lay still. The mind went into it, but speaking by speech, seeing by the eye, hearing by the ear, thinking by the mind, it lay still. Then breath went into it, and thence it rose at once. All these deities, having recognized the preeminence in life, and having comprehended life alone as the conscious self, went out of this body with all these five different kinds of life, and rested in the air, knowing that life had entered the air and merged in the ether, they went to heaven. And in the same manner, he who knows this, having recognized the preëminence in prâna, and having comprehended life alone as the conscious self, goes out of this body with all these, does no longer believe in this body, and resting in the air, and merged in the ether, he goes to heaven: he goes to where those gods are. And having reached this heaven, he, who knows this, becomes immortal with that immortality which those gods enjoy.

"Next follows the father's tradition to the son, and thus they explain it. The father, when going to depart, calls his son, after having strewn the house with fresh grass, having laid the sacrificial fire, and having placed near it a pot of water with a jug, full of rice, himself covered with a new cloth, and dressed in white. He places himself above his son, touching his organs with his organs, or he may deliver the tradition to him while he sits before him. Then he delivers it to him. The father says: 'Let me place my speech in the.' The son says: 'I take thy speech in me.' The father says: 'Let me place my scent in thee.' The son says: 'I take thy scent in me.' The father says: 'Let me place my eye in the.' The son says: 'I take thy eye in me.' The father says: 'Let me place my ear in the.' The son says: 'I take thy ear in me.' The father says: 'Let me place my tastes of food in the.' The son says: 'I take thy tastes of food in me.' The father says: 'Let me place my actions in the.' The son says: 'I take thy actions in me.' The father says: 'Let me place my pleasure and pain in the.' The son says: 'I take thy pleasure and pain in me.' The father says: 'Let me place happiness, joy, and offspring in thee.' The son says: 'I take thy happiness, joy, and offspring in me.' The father says: 'Let me place my walking in the.' The son says: 'I take thy walking in me.' The father says: 'Let me place my mind in the.' The son says: 'I take thy mind in me.' The father says: 'Let me place my knowledge in the.' The son says: 'I take thy knowledge in me.' But if the father is very ill, he may say shortly: Let me place my spirits in thee,' and the son: 'I take thy spirits in me.'

"The son then turns around to face his father while keeping his right side facing him and walks away. "May fame, the splendor of countenance, and honor always follow thee," the father cries after him. The other than turns to face him and says, "Obtain the celestial worlds and all desires," while covering his left shoulder with a hand or the hem of his clothing.

"If the father recovers, either places him under his son's rule or allows him to live a hermit's life. However, if he leaves, let them properly dispatch him, indeed.

LIVING AND BEING CONSCIOUS

The son of King of Kasî Divodâsa, Pratardana arrived in

Indra's beautiful home via battle and power. Pratardana, I'll offer you a boon to pick from, Indra stated. Pratardana responded, "Do you select that boon for me that you consider being most advantageous for a man?" "No one who chooses picks for another; choose thyself," Indra advised him. "Then that ability to choose is no boon for me," Pratardana retorted.

Then, however, Indra did not swerve from the truth, for Indra is truth. Indra said to him: "Know me only; that is what I deem most beneficial for man, that he should know me. I slew the three-headed son of Tvashtri; I delivered the Arunmukhas, the devotees, to the wolves; breaking many treaties, I killed the people of Prahlâda in heaven, the people of Puloma in the sky, the people of Kâlakañga on earth. And not one hair of me was harmed there. And he who knows me thus, by no deed of his is his life harmed: not by the murder of his mother, not by the murder of his father, not by theft, not by the killing of a Brahman. If he is going to sin, the bloom does not depart from his face. I am prâna, meditate on me as the conscious self, as life, as immortality. Life is prâna, prâna is life. Immortality is prâna, prâna is immortality. As long as prâna dwells in this body, so long surely there is life. By prâna, he obtains immortality in the other world, by knowledge true conception. He who meditates on me as life and immortality gains his full life in this world, and obtains in the Svarga world immortality and indestructibility."

Pratardana said: "Some maintain here, that the prânas become one, for otherwise no one could at the same time make known a name by speech, see a form with the eye, hear a sound with the ear, think a thought with the mind. After having become one, the prânas perceive all these together, one by one. While speech speaks, all prânas speak after it. While the eye sees, all prânas see after it. While the ear hears, all prânas hear after it. While the mind thinks, all prânas think after it. While the prâna breathes, all prânas breathe after it."

"Thus it is indeed," said Indra, "nevertheless there is a preëminence among the prânas. Man lives deprived of speech, for we see dumb people. Man lives deprived of sight, for we see blind people. Man lives deprived of hearing, for we see deaf people. Man lives deprived of mind, for we see infants. Man lives deprived of his arms, deprived of his legs, for we see it thus. But prâna alone is the conscious self and having laid hold of this body, it makes it rise. Therefore it is said, 'Let man worship it alone as uktha.' What is prâna, that is pragñâ, or self-consciousness; what is pragñâ (self-consciousness), that is prâna, for together they live in this body, and together they go out of it. Of that, this is the evidence, this is the understanding. When a man, being thus asleep, sees no dream whatever he becomes one with that prâna alone. Then speech goes to him when he is absorbed in prâna, with all names, the eye with all forms, the ear with all sounds, the mind with all thoughts. And when he awakes, then, as from a burning fire sparks proceed in all directions; thus from that self the prânas proceed, each towards its place: from the prânas the gods, from the gods the worlds.

"Of this, this is the proof, this is the understanding. When a man is thus sick, going to die, falling into weakness and faintness, they say: 'His thought has departed, he hears not, he sees not, he speaks not, he thinks not.' Then he becomes one with that prâna alone. Then speech goes to him who is absorbed in prâna, with all names, the eye with all forms, the ear with all sounds, the mind with all thoughts. And when he departs from this body, he departs together with all these.

"Speech gives up to him who is absorbed in prâna all names so that by a speech he obtains all names. The nose gives up to him all odors so that by scent he obtains all odors. The eye gives up to him all forms so that by the eye he obtains all forms. The ear gives up to him all sounds so that by the ear he obtains all sounds. The mind gives up to him all thoughts so that by the mind he obtains all thoughts. This is the complete absorption in prâna. And what is prâna is pragñâ, or self-consciousness; what is pragñâ, is prâna. For together do these two live in the body, and together do they depart.

"Now we shall explain how all things become one in that self-consciousness. Speech is one portion taken out of pragñâ, or self-conscious knowledge: the word is its object, placed outside. The nose is one portion taken out of it, the odor is its object, placed outside. The eye is one portion taken out of it, the form is its object, placed outside. The ear is one portion taken out of it, the sound is its object, placed outside. The tongue is one portion taken out of it, the taste of food is its object, placed outside. The two hands are one portion taken out of it, their action is their object, placed outside. The body is one portion taken out of it, its pleasure and pain are its objects, placed outside. The organ is one portion taken out of it, happiness, joy, and offspring are its object, placed outside. The two feet are one portion taken out of it, movements are their object, placed outside. Mind is one portion taken out of it, thoughts and desires are its objects, placed outside.

"Having by self-conscious knowledge taken possession of speech, he obtains by speech all words. Having taken possession of the nose, he obtains all odors. Having taken possession of the eye, he obtains all forms. Having taken possession of the ear, he obtains all sounds. Having taken possession of the tongue, he obtains all tastes of food. Having taken possession of the two hands, he obtains all actions. Having taken possession of the body, he obtains pleasure and pain. Having taken possession of the organ, he obtains happiness, joy, and offspring. Having taken possession of the two feet, he obtains all movements. Having taken possession of the mind, he obtains all thoughts.

"For without self-consciousness speech does not make known to the self any word. 'My mind was absent,' he says, 'I did not perceive that word.' Without self-consciousness, the nose does not make known any odor. 'My mind was absent,' he says, 'I did not perceive that odor.' Without self-consciousness, the eye does not make known any form. 'My mind was absent,' he says, 'I did not perceive that form.' Without self-consciousness, the ear does not make known any sound. 'My mind was absent,' he says, 'I did not perceive that sound.' Without self-consciousness, the tongue does not make known any taste. 'My mind was absent,' he says, 'I did not perceive that taste.' Without self-consciousness, the two hands do not make known any act. 'Our mind was absent,' they say, 'we did not perceive any act.' Without self-consciousness, the body does not make known pleasure or pain. 'My mind was absent,' he says, 'I did not perceive that pleasure or pain.' Without self-consciousness, the organ does not make known happiness, joy, or offspring. 'My mind was absent,' he says, 'I did not perceive that happiness, joy, or offspring.' Without self-consciousness, the two feet do not make known any movement. 'Our mind was absent,' they say, 'we did not perceive that movement.' Without self-consciousness no thought succeeds, nothing can be known that is to be known.

"Let no man try to find out what speech is, let him know the speaker. Let no man try to find out what odor is, let him know who smells. Let no man try to find out what form is, let him know the seer. Let no man try to find out what sound is, let him know the hearer. Let no man try to find out the tastes of food, let him know the knower of tastes. Let no man try to find out what action is, let him know the agent. Let no man try to find out what pleasure and pain are, let him know the knower of pleasure and pain. Let no man try to find out what happiness, joy, and offspring are, let him know the knower of happiness, joy, and offspring. Let no man try to find out what movement is, let him know the mover. Let no man try to find out what the mind is, let him know the thinker. These ten objects (what is spoken, smelled, seen, felt) have to reference self-consciousness; the ten subjects (speech, the senses, mind) have reference to objects. If there were no objects, there would be no subjects; and if there were no subjects, there would be no objects. For on either side alone nothing could be achieved. But the self of pragñâ, consciousness, and prâna, life, is not many, but one. For as in a car, the circumference of a wheel is placed on the spokes, and the spokes on the nave, thus are these objects, as a circumference, placed on the subjects as spokes, and the subjects on the prâna. And that prâna, the living, and breathing power, indeed is the self of pragñâ, the self-conscious self: blessed, imperishable, immortal. He does not increase by a good action, nor decrease by a bad actor. For the self of prâna and pragñâ makes him, whom he wishes to lead up from these worlds, do a good deed; and the same makes him, whom he wishes to lead down from these worlds, do a bad deed. And he is the guardian of the world, he is the king of the world, he is the lord of the universe-- and he is my (Indra's) self; thus let it be known, yea, thus let it be known!"

[Footnote 14: The question Kitra posed to Svetaketu was extremely cryptic and was likely written with obscurity in mind from the start. Without a doubt, Kitra wanted to inquire about the afterlife.

There are two ways to enter this future life: one leads to the world of Brahman (the conditioned), beyond which there is only one more stage, which is represented by knowledge of and identity with the unconditioned Brahman, and the other leads to the world of the fathers, from where it is possible to return to this world after the reward for doing good deeds has been used up. Worms, insects, and other living things on the ground have a third route, but they are of little importance. It is now abundantly evident that King Kitra knows something about the two pathways beyond death—sometimes referred to as the right and left, the southern and northern roads—that Svetaketu does not. The southern or right route, also known as the path of the fathers, continues from smoke and night to the dark half of the moon, while the northern or left road, also known as the path of the Devas, travels from light and day to the bright half of the moon.

Therefore, both paths come together on the moon before splitting apart. While the southern route passes by the six months when the sun moves towards the south, to the world of the fathers, the ether, and the moon, the northern road passes by the six months when the sun moves towards the north, through the sun, moon, and lightning to the world of Brahman. The major distinction between the two routes is that although individuals who take the former do not continually return to earthly existence but instead arrive at a true understanding of the unconditioned Brahmân, those who take the latter route do so repeatedly, returning to earth to experience fresh births.

While the Brahmans focused more on what may be called the shorter cut, knowledge of Brahman as the actual Self, the royal families of India seem to have been the only ones who speculated about what would happen to the soul after death. With them, knowing meant to be, and as the body disintegrated, they anticipated immediate liberation from all wanderings.]

Who is aware of the conditioned and mythical form of Brahman portrayed here, lounging on the couch? [Footnote 15]

[Footnote 16: He approaches the couch, Amitaugas, which is prâna, as stated in the first chapter (breath, spirit, life). As a result, after explaining the knowledge of the couch (of Brahman) in the first chapter, the next topic to be explained is the knowledge of prâna, the living spirit, which was briefly mistaken for Brahman or the ultimate cause of everything.]

[Footnote 17: Speech requires visual verification since it is erratic. The ear must be used to verify the sight because it misinterprets the mother of pearl for silver. Because the mind must be alert for the ear to hear, the ear is unreliable and must be monitored by the mind. Finally, as there is no mind without spirit, the mind is dependent on the spirit.

[Footnote 18] Because a man will give up all to protect his vital spirits or his life, the vital spirits are referred to as the highest treasure.

[Footnote 19] This is one of the earliest, if not the earliest, references to the sacred string known as the yagopavîta, which is worn over the left shoulder during sacrifices.

[Footnote 20: Professor Cowell has translated an intriguing passage from the commentary that demonstrates how the Upanishads' and the commentary's authors both had a good understanding of the correlative nature of knowledge. He claims that the organ of sense cannot exist without pragmatism (self-consciousness), , nor the objects of sense be acquired without the organ, therefore—on the theory that when one thing cannot exist without another, that thing is said to be identical with the other—as, for example, the cloth, being never perceived without the threads, is identical with them, or the (false perception of) silver, being never found without the mother of pearl, is identical with it, so the objects of sense being never acquired without the organs are identical with them, an, nor the objects of sense be acquired without the organ, therefore—on the theory that when one thing cannot exist without another, that thing is said to be identical with the other—as, for example, the cloth, being never perceived without the threads, is identical with them, or the (false perception of) silver, being never found without the mother of pearl, is identical with it, so the objects of sense being never acquired without the organs are identical with them, an

www.ingramcontent.com/pod-product-compliance
Lightning Source LLC
Chambersburg PA
CBHW020856160726

47993CB00004B/1684